Francis Frith's
AROUND LIVERPOOL

◆

PHOTOGRAPHIC MEMORIES

Francis Frith's
AROUND LIVERPOOL

◆

Clive Hardy

British Library Cataloguing in Publication Data

Around Liverpool
Clive Hardy
ISBN 1-85937-051-9

Frith Book Company Ltd
Frith's Barn, Teffont,
Salisbury, Wiltshire SP3 5QP
Tel: +44 (0) 1722 716 376
Email: info@frithbook.co.uk
www.frithbook.co.uk

Printed and bound in Great Britain

CONTENTS

Francis Frith: Victorian Pioneer   7

Frith's Archive - A Unique Legacy   10

Liverpool - An Introduction   12

The City   18

To Widnes and Warrington   46

The Wirral Side of the River   53

West Bank Villages   78

Index   83

Free Mounted Print Voucher   87

FRANCIS FRITH: *Victorian Pioneer*

FRANCIS FRITH, Victorian founder of the world-famous photographic archive, was a complex and multitudinous man. A devout Quaker and a highly successful Victorian businessman, he was both philosophic by nature and pioneering in outlook.

By 1855 Francis Frith had already established a wholesale grocery business in Liverpool, and sold it for the astonishing sum of £200,000, which is the equivalent today of over £15,000,000. Now a multi-millionaire, he was able to indulge his passion for travel. As a child he had pored over travel books written by early explorers, and his fancy and imagination had been stirred by family holidays to the sublime mountain regions of Wales and Scotland. 'What a land of spirit-stirring and enriching scenes and places!' he had written. He was to return to these scenes of grandeur in later years to 'recapture the thousands of vivid and tender memories', but with a different purpose. Now in his thirties, and captivated by the new science of photography, Frith set out on a series of pioneering journeys to the Nile regions that occupied him from 1856 until 1860.

INTRIGUE AND ADVENTURE

He took with him on his travels a specially-designed wicker carriage that acted as both dark-room and sleeping chamber. These far-flung journeys were packed with intrigue and adventure. In his life story, written when he was sixty-three, Frith tells of being held captive by bandits, and of fighting 'an awful midnight battle to the very point of surrender with a deadly pack of hungry, wild dogs'. Sporting flowing Arab costume, Frith arrived at Akaba by camel seventy years before Lawrence, where he encountered 'desert princes and rival sheikhs, blazing with jewel-hilted swords'.

During these extraordinary adventures he was assiduously exploring the desert regions bordering the Nile and patiently recording the antiquities and peoples with his camera. He was the first photographer to venture beyond the sixth cataract. Africa was still the mysterious 'Dark Continent', and Stanley and Livingstone's historic meeting was a decade into the future. The conditions for picture taking confound belief. He laboured for hours in his wicker dark-room in the sweltering heat of the desert, while the volatile chemicals fizzed dangerously in their trays. Often he was forced to work in remote tombs and caves where conditions were cooler. Back in London he exhibited his photographs and was 'rapturously cheered' by members of the Royal Society. His reputation as a photographer was made overnight. An eminent modern historian has likened their impact on the population of the time to that on our own generation of the first photographs taken on the surface of the moon.

VENTURE OF A LIFE-TIME

Characteristically, Frith quickly spotted the opportunity to create a new business as a specialist publisher of photographs. He lived in an era of immense and sometimes violent change. For the poor in the early part of Victoria's reign work was a drudge and the hours long, and people had precious little free time to enjoy themselves.

Most had no transport other than a cart or gig at their disposal, and had not travelled far beyond the boundaries of their own town or village. However, by the 1870s, the railways had threaded their way across the country, and Bank Holidays and half-day Saturdays had been made obligatory by Act of Parliament. All of a sudden the ordinary working man and his family were able to enjoy days out and see a little more of the world.

With characteristic business acumen, Francis Frith foresaw that these new tourists would enjoy having souvenirs to commemorate their days out. In 1860 he married Mary Ann Rosling and set out with the intention of photographing every city, town and village in Britain. For the next thirty years he travelled the country by train and by pony and trap, producing fine photographs of seaside resorts and beauty spots that were keenly bought by millions of Victorians. These prints were painstakingly pasted into family albums and pored over during the dark nights of winter, rekindling precious memories of summer excursions.

THE RISE OF FRITH & CO

Frith's studio was soon supplying retail shops all over the country. To meet the demand he gathered about him a small team of photographers, and published the work of independent artist-photographers of the calibre of Roger Fenton and Francis Bedford. In order to gain some understanding of the scale of Frith's business one only has to look at the catalogue issued by Frith & Co in 1886: it runs to some 670

pages, listing not only many thousands of views of the British Isles but also many photographs of most European countries, and China, Japan, the USA and Canada – note the sample page shown above from the hand-written *Frith & Co* ledgers detailing pictures taken. By 1890 Frith had created the greatest specialist photographic publishing company in the world, with over 2,000 outlets – more than the combined number that Boots and WH Smith have today! The picture on the right shows the *Frith & Co* display board at Ingleton in the Yorkshire Dales. Beautifully constructed with mahogany frame and gilt inserts, it could display up to a dozen local scenes.

POSTCARD BONANZA

The ever-popular holiday postcard we know today took many years to develop. In 1870 the Post Office issued the first plain cards, with a pre-printed stamp on one face. In 1894 they allowed other publishers' cards to be sent through the mail with an attached adhesive halfpenny stamp. Demand grew rapidly, and in 1895 a new size of postcard was permitted called the

court card, but there was little room for illustration. In 1899, a year after Frith's death, a new card measuring 5.5 x 3.5 inches became the standard format, but it was not until 1902 that the divided back came into being, with address and message on one face and a full-size illustration on the other. *Frith & Co* were in the vanguard of postcard development, and Frith's sons Eustace and Cyril continued their father's monumental task, expanding the number of views offered to the public and recording more and more places in Britain, as the coasts and countryside were opened up to mass travel.

Francis Frith died in 1898 at his villa in Cannes, his great project still growing. The archive he created continued in business for another seventy years. By 1970 it contained over a third of a million pictures of 7,000 cities, towns and villages. The massive photographic record Frith has left to us stands as a living monument to a special and very remarkable man.

Frith's Archive: *A Unique Legacy*

FRANCIS FRITH'S legacy to us today is of immense significance and value, for the magnificent archive of evocative photographs he created provides a unique record of change in 7,000 cities, towns and villages throughout Britain over a century and more. Frith and his fellow studio photographers revisited locations many times down the years to update their views, compiling for us an enthralling and colourful pageant of British life and character.

We tend to think of Frith's sepia views of Britain as nostalgic, for most of us use them to conjure up memories of places in our own lives with which we have family associations. It often makes us forget that to Francis Frith they were records of daily life as it was actually being lived in the cities, towns and villages of his day. The Victorian age was one of great and often bewildering change for ordinary people, and though the pictures evoke an impression of slower times, life was as busy and hectic as it is today.

We are fortunate that Frith was a photographer of the people, dedicated to recording the minutiae of everyday life. For it is this sheer wealth of visual data, the painstaking chronicle of changes in dress, transport, street layouts, buildings, housing, engineering and landscape that captivates us so much today. His remarkable images offer us a powerful link with the past and with the lives of our ancestors.

TODAY'S TECHNOLOGY

Computers have now made it possible for Frith's many thousands of images to be accessed almost instantly. In the Frith archive today, each photograph is carefully 'digitised' then stored on a CD Rom. Frith archivists can locate a single photograph amongst thousands within seconds. Views can be catalogued and sorted under a variety of categories of place and content to the immediate benefit of researchers. Inexpensive reference prints can be created for them at the touch of a mouse button, and a wide range of books and other printed materials assembled and published for a wider, more general readership - in the next twelve months over a hundred Frith local history titles will be published! The

See Frith at www. francisfrith.co.uk

day-to-day workings of the archive are very different from how they were in Francis Frith's time: imagine the herculean task of sorting through eleven tons of glass negatives as Frith had to do to locate a particular sequence of pictures! Yet the archive still prides itself on maintaining the same high standards of excellence laid down by Francis Frith, including the painstaking cataloguing and indexing of every view.

It is curious to reflect on how the internet now allows researchers in America and elsewhere greater instant access to the archive than Frith himself ever enjoyed. Many thousands of individual views can be called up on screen within seconds on one of the Frith internet sites, enabling people living continents away to revisit the streets of their ancestral home town, or view places in Britain where they have enjoyed holidays. Many overseas researchers welcome the chance to view special theme selections, such as transport, sports, costume and ancient monuments.

We are certain that Francis Frith would have heartily approved of these modern developments, for he himself was always working at the very limits of Victorian photographic technology.

THE VALUE OF THE ARCHIVE TODAY

Because of the benefits brought by the computer, Frith's images are increasingly studied by social historians, by researchers into genealogy and ancestory, by architects, town planners, and by teachers and schoolchildren involved in local history projects. In addition, the archive offers every one of us a unique opportunity to examine the places where we and our families have lived and worked down the years. Immensely successful in Frith's own era, the archive is now, a century and more on, entering a new phase of popularity.

THE PAST IN TUNE WITH THE FUTURE

Historians consider the Francis Frith Collection to be of prime national importance. It is the only archive of its kind remaining in private ownership and has been valued at a million pounds. However, this figure is now rapidly increasing as digital technology enables more and more people around the world to enjoy its benefits.

Francis Frith's archive is now housed in an historic timber barn in the beautiful village of Teffont in Wiltshire. Its founder would not recognize the archive office as it is today. In place of the many thousands of dusty boxes containing glass plate negatives and an all-pervading odour of photographic chemicals, there are now ranks of computer screens. He would be amazed to watch his images travelling round the world at unimaginable speeds through network and internet lines.

The archive's future is both bright and exciting. Francis Frith, with his unshakeable belief in making photographs available to the greatest number of people, would undoubtedly approve of what is being done today with his lifetime's work. His photographs, depicting our shared past, are now bringing pleasure and enlightenment to millions around the world a century and more after his death.

LIVERPOOL – *An Introduction*

IN 1086 WHEN the Domesday Book was being compiled, Liverpool, if anything of it existed at all, was so insignificant that it failed to get a mention. The nearest place of any consequence was West Derby, with its motte and bailey castle. By the beginning of the 13th century the garrison consisted of ten knights and 140 men-at-arms. It was in 1207 that a township was founded on the banks of the Mersey by King John, but it did not rate as a parish, because its inhabitants had to attend church at Walton-on-the-Hill some three miles away. John is thought to have granted it rights to hold a weekly market and an annual fair, as well as to build a mill. The earliest streets ran west to east and were Bank Street, Dale Street, Chapel Street and Moor Street. They were connected by Juggler Street, which extended north to form Oldhall Street, and south to make Castle Street.

For the next four centuries or so the town would grow slowly, with little development beyond its original layout. Apart from the royal manor at West Derby, the other important area was Toxteth. Here, there was a royal chase that had probably been established in the 12th century. John, however, redeveloped

it by wasting the manors of Toxteth and Smeedon to incorporate extra acreage. The chase is known to have been a large establishment with a staff of four master huntsmen and forty-nine men. They were responsible for two packs of dogs, 52 spaniels and 2000 hand nets.

Like his father, Henry II, and his brother, Richard, John was prepared to spend money on castles, with around 10 per cent of the Crown's annual income going on such projects. Most of the money went on maintaining and improving existing fortresses, but Liverpool was given a new one, perched on a rocky ledge from which it commanded the view of both town and fledgling port.

In 1642, during the Civil War, the castle was seized by the Royalists, but in May of the following year it fell to Parliament. In October the meeting of deputy lieutenants at Preston decided Parliament should maintain garrisons at both Liverpool and Warrington; this was the right move, considering the chaos caused in December when Royalist warships entered the Mersey. Fearing an assault on Liverpool, troops were ordered south from Preston and had got as far as Prescot before they found out the ships had gone.

In 1644 Prince Rupert captured Liverpool after a night attack, despite stiff resistance from its garrison. The Royalist gain was, however, short lived: after a ten-week seige, on 1 November it fell to the Parliamentary forces of Sir John Meldrum, and an attempt by Lord Byron to recapture it ended in disaster when his command was destroyed by Sir William Brereton. Liverpool remained in Parliament's hands until the end of the war.

Though the castle was never slighted, it was partly demolished between 1660 and 1678. In

holding centre for rebels awaiting transportation, as Sir Thomas John was paid £1000 in 1716 to transport 130 men from Liverpool to the West Indies. The thirty rebels who were put on board one ship managed to overpower the crew and sailed for France, where they sold the vessel and her cargo and divided the money between themselves.

SLAVERS AND PRIVATEERS

In 1701, just one Liverpool ship of thirty tons was engaged in the Guinea trade, as slav-

the aftermath of the Jacobite Rebellion of 1715 the Tower of Liverpool was used as a place of confinement for rebels taken at Preston, of whom sixty-six were convicted of high treason. Of these, twenty-two were executed, including four in Liverpool at Gallows Mill. Many of the accused were offered a deal whereby, if they pleaded guilty to taking part in the rebellion, they would be sentenced to transportation; those who insisted on pleading not guilty were told that they would face the death penalty if convicted.

The Tower appears to have been used as a

ing was then called. Bristol and London ships dominated the business. By 1730 Liverpool had fifteen slavers totalling 1,111 tons, and by 1771 the figure had risen to 105 ships totalling 10,929 tons. The American War of Independence saw a decline in the number of ships engaged in the traffic of slaving; in 1779, just eleven vessels were involved. But with the end of the conflict, it was soon business as usual. By 1785 there were 79 ships, but the largest number in any one year was in 1798 when 149 vessels totalling 34,937 tons carried 53,051 slaves. By the end of the 18th century

Liverpool had eclipsed both Bristol and London to become the country's main slave port.

The slavers did not always have it their own way. One morning in September 1799 the 'Thomas' was on her way to Barbados with a cargo of 375 slaves. The ship's crew was at breakfast, but several female slaves had noticed that the arms chest was open. While the crew ate, the women passed the guns to the male slaves, who then rushed the crew's quarters. Captain Peter M'Quie and many of his crew were killed in the fighting. Twelve managed to get away in the stern boat, but of these, only two would survive to make it to Barbados. Several others got away in the long-boat and made it to Watling's Island in the Bahamas. The five surviving crewmen on board the 'Thomas' were kept alive by the slaves to work the ship, and it would be 42 days later before they too could escape. An American brigantine loaded with rum came alongside the 'Thomas' and was taken by the slaves, though her crew managed to get away in their boat. The slaves then decided to cele-brate their victory by going on a binge and getting drunk on rum. The five captive crew-men were then able to retake the brig and make for Long Island, Providence. The slaves were left on the deep blue sea until they were intercepted by HMS 'Thames'.

During the American War of Independence it is thought a few privateers were fitted out at Liverpool. However, war with the French was always different. Between August 1778 and April 1779 no less than 120 ships sailed under letters of marque.

Slaving and privateering were not the only trades that Liverpool ships were involved in. In 1750 the 'Golden Lion', a former French prize, made the first whaling voyage from the port. By 1790 there were twenty ships engaged in the Greenland trade; to encour-age whaling, Parliament enacted to exclude the crews of whaling ships from being press-ganged into the Royal Navy. There are instances of seamen armed with harpoons and vicious looking whaling knives going along to Liverpool's customs house to collect their certificates of exemption. The certifi-

cates were valid for the whaling season or until a voyage was completed. In 1752 there were 357 vessels belonging to Liverpool, of which about fifty were engaged in slaving. There were a further eighty river vessels, mainly operating the salt traffic between Liverpool and Northwich. By the 1760s, Liverpool was handling more ships than Bristol. In 1764 the port handled 766 inbound and 823 outbound vessels, compared to Bristol's figures of 332 inbound and 343 outbound.

OTHER VENTURES

By the early 1760s, Liverpool had 117 potters at work, and with the ease with which China clay could be brought by sea from Cornwall, the town could, and should, have given the Potteries a run for its money. However, the local potters seem to have preferred to use the local clay they could get from the common, and being unable to compete with Delft ware, which was the fashionable thing, the industry had all but collapsed by 1768.

Liverpool in the 18th century could at least boast some excellent clock and watch makers. In 1758, John Wykes opened a clock works on the site later occupied by the Police Court. Henry Hardman, who was active between 1767 and 1773, produced some of the finest grandfather clocks in the country. Peter Litherland was the man who invented a watch that could beat seconds and the rack escapement.

In 1770 the port landed its first cargo of cotton from the West Indies and the American colonies. It comprised 6,037 bags, three barrels and three bales of cotton. By the 1850s, the trade had grown to more than 2 million packages a year, of which at least 1.7 million were from the United States. With all this cotton coming through the port, you would have thought that Liverpool itself would have become a major centre for cotton spinning. In 1796 a mill was opened by Thomas Middleton in Cheapside, but it burnt down. Kirkham & Co opened a mill for spinning cotton-twist, and Edward Pemberton established a spinning mill in Bolton Street, yet both of these businesses closed down. The last fling came in 1839 when a mill opened at Canal Bank, but it too went the way of Middleton's establishment and burnt down in May 1853.

By the last quarter of the 18th century Liverpool had surpassed Bristol as a port, but even so it was still a moderate-sized place. In 1775 there were only three docks, while on the south side of Church Street there was a large orchard. Bold Street did not exist, and

Clayton Square consisted of just a few houses. The combined population of the town and parish was no more than 35,000. There were only two houses at Edge Hill, and the built-up part of Liverpool terminated in the north at Oldhall Street, to the south at the lower ends of Park Lane and Pitt Street, and to the east at Whitechapel and Church Street.

One of the more unusual entries in Kaye's 'Stranger in Liverpool', published in 1823, concerns the floating baths, launched in June 1816 and moored opposite George's Dock Parade. The vessel was 82ft long by 34ft wide on the deck, and was said to combine the comfort of cleanliness and convenience. Kaye states that 'the bath is a reservoir, 80 feet long by 27 feet wide, and has a current of water continually flowing through it by means of four sluices at each end of the floor of the vessel; the depth of water is graduated by the slope of the floor of the bath, from six feet to three feet and a half. On each side of the vessel, where the current passes out, are two private baths, with a dressing-room to each,

where the bather remains totally unseen: those who prefer bathing in the river, pass through a door on the outside of the vessel, so that the persons of the bathers are not exposed to the spectators on shore'.

THE MANCHESTER SHIP CANAL

That the Manchester Ship Canal was built at all is owing to the enthusiasm of one man, Daniel Adamson, the owner of an engineering works at Dukinfield. He invited councillors and leading businessmen to his home in Didsbury, where he put forward the proposal for the Ship Canal. In 1877, and again in 1881, Hamilton Fulton had suggested that Manchester could be linked to the Mersey by means of a tidal canal. The major disadvantage was that Manchester Docks would have been built at the bottom of a very deep hole, as the city is over sixty feet above sea level. Why was the canal needed? It appears that during the 1870s both the Mersey Docks & Harbour Board and the railways in the north

west were taking advantage of the popularity of Liverpool to hike their prices for freight handling and forwarding, and Manchester-based businesses were more than a little displeased. Adamson's scheme for a canal found favour, and received backing from local authorities and chambers of commerce. However, the Mersey Docks & Harbour Board and the railways were wealthy enough to ensure that the first two bills were killed off, but the third bill, which altered the entrance to the canal from Runcorn to further along the river at Eastham, received the royal assent. Work began in 1887, and was completed in 1894, at a cost of £15 million.

Sited on the Wirral side of the river, with the largest weekly market in the Wirral, and the roads from five neighbouring villages meeting there, Upton was once an important place. The village grew with the coming of the railways in general, and a link with the Mersey Railway in particular, making it an attractive place to live for those wealthy enough to escape from Liverpool. In 1931 the village had to vote as to which local authority it would join. Both Wallasey and Birkenhead were keen and undertook a considerable amount of campaigning in order to woo the locals. With polling day set for 10 March, Wallasey chose the 9th to play what it believed to be its trump card. With bell ringing, a Wallasey fire engine turned up in the village sporting a banner 'WE CAN REACH ANY FIRE IN UPTON IN TEN MINUTES'. Within minutes one of the pro-Birkenhead villagers had reported back with the result that Birkenhead sent its very latest appliance over to Upton bearing an even larger banner 'WHY WAIT TEN MINUTES TO HAVE YOUR FIRE PUT OUT WHEN WE CAN DO IT IN FOUR?' Needless to say Birkenhead got the votes.

LIME STREET 1890   26661

ST NICHOLAS' PLACE, 1895 36660
The floating bridge and landing stage was opened in 1876. At 2,450ft in length, and supported on 200 iron pontoons the landing stage, is claimed to be the largest floating structure in the world. The north end, or Prince's stage, was used by sea-going ships whilst the southern, or George's stage, was used by the river ferries.

THE OVERHEAD RAILWAY 1895 36658

The Tower Buildings were built on the site of the Tower of Liverpool, which was used as the local gaol until 1811. In the 1750s it even housed French prisoners of war. In 1715 it was used to confine Jacobite rebels taken at Preston. Sixty-six men were convicted of high treason, of whom twenty-two were executed, including four at nearby Gallows Mill.

GEORGE'S DOCK C1881 14149

George's Dock was excavated from land given by the Corporation. There were problems with the Old Dock due to silting, and in 1736 it had to be closed for six months for cleaning. In 1737 the decision was taken to build Salthouse Dock, but by 1748 it was already too small to take the larger merchant ships which were then being built.

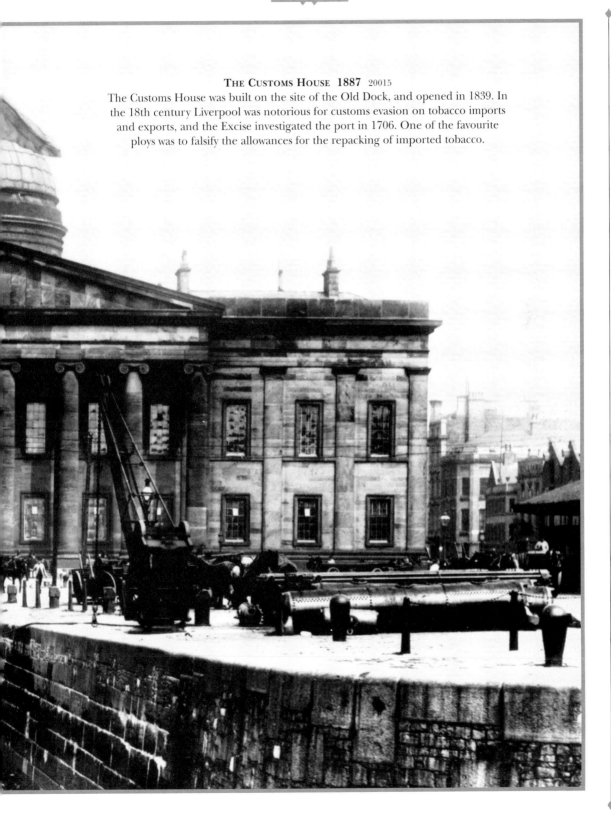

THE CUSTOMS HOUSE 1887 20015
The Customs House was built on the site of the Old Dock, and opened in 1839. In the 18th century Liverpool was notorious for customs evasion on tobacco imports and exports, and the Excise investigated the port in 1706. One of the favourite ploys was to falsify the allowances for the repacking of imported tobacco.

THE ROYAL LIVER BUILDING c1955 L60019
George's Dock was built on land given by the Corporation, but when it was filled in, the site was occupied by the
headquarters of the Mersey Docks & Harbour Board, the Cunard Building, and the Royal Liver Insurance Building.

CHURCH STREET c1890 L60001

During the late 18th century Church Street was a residential area. Here lived surgeon Richard Gerard, who was mayor in 1780, George Case, who was mayor in 1781, and the merchants Henry Midgley, Henry Clay, Thomas Holding, Edward Forbes and George Rowden.

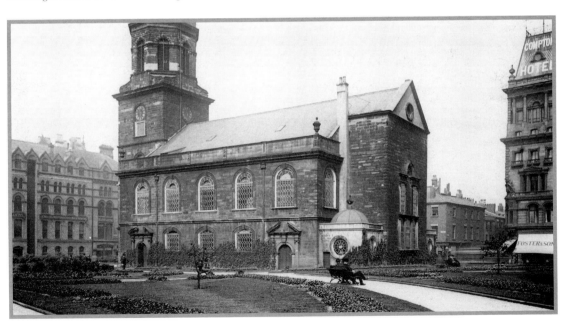

THE CATHEDRAL 1890 26665

The Cathedral Church of St Peter was erected as a result of Liverpool being made a parish in its own right in 1699. The Act of Separation directed that a parish church and churchyard were to be provided, with the result that St Peter's was consecrated in 1704. The picture was taken before the pinnacles were added to each angle of the octagonal tower.

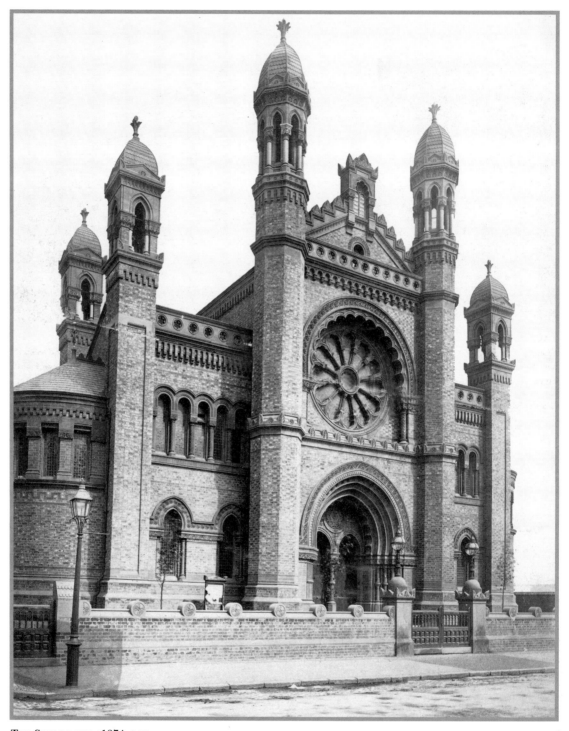

THE SYNAGOGUE c1874 7421

The earliest synagogue in Liverpool was situated at the lower end of Cumberland Street, but later moved to a building on the south side of the Old Dock, and later still to Upper Frederick Street. In 1808 a new synagogue opened in Seel Street, and a second was later opened in Pilgrim Street.

ST GEORGE'S HALL C1881 7813

St George's Hall, one of the finest neo-classical buildings in Europe, was opened in 1854. In common with many civic buildings in the 1830s, the design was chosen by means of a competition; in this instance the winner was Harvey Lonsdale Elmes.

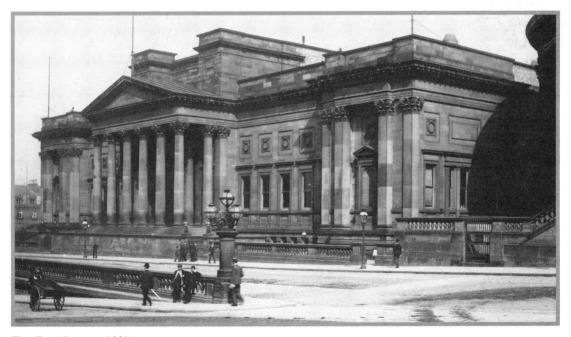

THE FREE LIBRARY 1895 36649

The Brown Library and Museum was designed by Thomas Allom and John Weightman, and was opened in 1860. It was the first specially-built public library in Britain, and is named after Sir William Brown, a wealthy cotton merchant, who paid for its construction and initial stock of books.

THE QUADRANT 1890 26662
Lime Street Station and the North Western Hotel. Lime Street was the main station for London & North Western services to London, Manchester, Edinburgh and Glasgow. The hotel was at the top end of the price scale, along with the Adelphi and the Lancashire & Yorkshire Hotel at Exchange Station. In 1906, rooms at these hotels started from 4s 6d a night; dinner from 5s.

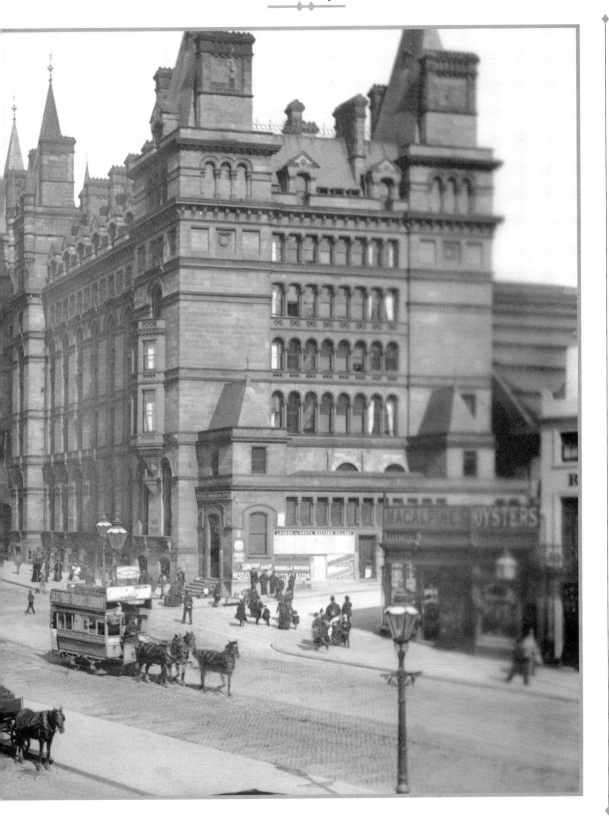

THE PICTON READING ROOM 1895 36648
Built between 1875-79, the circular Picton Library was designed by Cornelius Sherlock and is named after Sir James Allanson Picton, first chairman of the Liverpool Libraries Committee.

THE ART GALLERY 1895 36647
The Walker Art Gallery was erected in 1877 by Sir Andrew Walker, and housed modern pictures, as well as a collection of early Italian, German and Flemish works. There were cartoons by Romney and Gibson and a sketch by Tintoretto.

THE SESSIONS HOUSE 1887 19995
Situated next door to the Walker Art Gallery, the Sessions House was built as a replacement for the one demolished to make way for the new Exchange building.

THE QUADRANT c1881 14071
Here we see the eastern facade of St George's Hall on
the left and Lime Street station on the right. In the
background are the Walker Art Gallery and the
County Sessions House. Rising above them is the
Wellington Monument.

COMMUTATION ROW 1895 36645
A closer look at the area around the Wellington Monument. The County Sessions House is the classical building on the left with the Corinthian portico. The junction of Lime Street and London Road is on the right; Islington Road is hidden behind the monument.

THE EXCHANGE 1895 36655
By 1862 the old Exchange building was too small for the volume of business being done there. The owners declined to become involved in a larger scheme, with the result that a new company was formed to push things through Parliament. They obtained an act to buy out the owners, pull down the Exchange and build something more befitting Britain's second port.

THE TOWN HALL 1895 36650

The Town Hall was originally built in 1754. In those days it did not have a portico, balustrade and cupola, but a front of Corinthian columns supporting a pediment. On 18 January 1795 a fire destroyed much of the building including its original dome. It was rebuilt with a redesigned interior and topped off with a cupola; the balustrades and portico were later additions to the south front.

THE EXCHANGE 1887 20001

Members of the Liverpool Exchange gather in front of the building. The new Exchange, described as Flemish Renaissance, cost £220,000 to build. It cost £317,350 to buy out the old owners and a further £60,000 to buy the old Sessions House, which was then demolished and its site incorporated into the new structure.

THE ADELPHI HOTEL 1870 7841

The Adelphi Hotel stands in Ranelagh Street. By 1906 this was one of the top three hotels in the city, along with the North Western and the Lancashire & Yorkshire. Hot on their heels were the St George in Dale Street, the Imperial and the Grand.

DALE STREET 1895 36653
Looking towards the Municipal Buildings. In the early 18th century Dale Street was one of the places around the town where pottery and clay pipes were manufactured, as there was easy access to clay on the waste or common. By 1761 there were at least 117 potters at work in the town, but within eight years the industry had imploded, as it was unable to compete with the fashionable Delftware.

DALE STREET 1887 20002
The municipal offices, with its imposing pyramidal spire, was designed by borough surveyor John Weightman and his successor E T Robson. The only criticism made at the time of its completion was that it would have looked even grander had it been set back from the street by fifteen to twenty yards.

BOLD STREET 1887 20010

Looking south towards St Luke's. The foundation of St Luke's was laid in 1811, but work continued at a slow pace for years as it was being paid for by the Corporation. Bombed in 1941, the shell of the old church has been retained as a memorial to the city's losses during World War II.

THE ENTRANCE TO THE MERSEY TUNNEL c1955 L60002

As early as January 1825 a proposal was made to construct a tunnel under the Mersey, but it never got anywhere despite being revived on a number of occasions. Though Parliamentary powers were first obtained in 1869, work did not start until 1925; the tunnel opened in 1934.

THE SS 'PARIS', THE SMOKING ROOM 1890 25088
Inman Line's 'City of Paris' was ordered from J & G Thompson's Clydebank yard (later John Brown & Co). The 'City of Paris' was a three-funnelled passenger liner of 10,798 grt (gross registered tonnage), and was launched on 23 October 1888.

THE SS 'PARIS', THE LIBRARY 1890 25087
The 'City of Paris' and her sister, the 'City of New York', had accommodation for 540 first-class, 200 second-class, and 1,000 steerage passengers. They were the first twin-screw liners to see service on the Atlantic. Their high speed meant they were soon holders of the Blue Riband. The library looks comfortable and well-stocked.

THE SS 'ADRIATIC' 1890 24417

THE SS 'ADRIATIC' 1890
The White Star liner 'Adriatic' in the Mersey. Built by Harland & Wolff, Belfast, she was launched in October 1871 and made her maiden voyage to New York in April 1872. A few weeks later she lifted the record for the west-bound crossing of the Atlantic from Cunard's 'Scotia' with a speed of 14.52 knots. When built, she carried 50 first- and 800 third-class passengers.

HMS 'HERCULES' 1890
HMS Hercules was a centre-battery, iron-clad battleship. Designed in 1865 and completed in 1868, she was a regular visitor to Liverpool along with other units of the channel fleet. One problem was a lack of firepower at the bow and stern. She had to rely on just one 9-inch and two 7-inch guns, and even then there was the possibility of blast damage.

HMS 'HERCULES' 1890 24422

HMS 'BELLEISLE' 1890 24421

HMS Belleisle rides at anchor in the Mersey, resplendent in her Victorian livery of black hull, white upper-works, and yellow ochre masts and funnel. With a length of 245ft, and armed with four heavy guns and six quick-firing guns, 'Belleisle' and her near-sister 'Orion' could steam at a maximum speed of 8 knots.

THE FERRY BOATS c1955 L60021

These are the famous Mersey ferries. By the early 1820s the ferry service was steam operated. The 'Etna' used Queen's Dock; the 'Abbey', of Birkenhead and the 'Mersey', sailed from George's Dock. Other ferries were the 'Tranmere' on the Tranmere run, the 'Royal Mail', which ran to and from Woodside, and the 'Seacombe' which went to Seacombe and back.

KNOWSLEY HALL 1890 26668

Knowsley Hall, set in 2,000 acres of parkland, was the private residence of the Earls of Derby. Members of the royal family were often guests here during their visits to Liverpool. The twelfth Earl instigated the Derby horserace, and the fifteenth Earl was once offered the crown of Greece, but declined it.

SEFTON PARK 1895 36673

In October 1867, HRH the Duke of Cambridge reviewed the local volunteer forces at Sefton, but things did not go according to plan. Crowd control was a farce, and many of the spectators finished up amid the troops. The troops took part in a mock battle; reinforcements were no problem at all, as many of the spectators took a unilateral decision and joined in.

SEFTON PARK BRIDGE 1887 20050
Sefton Park was officially opened by Prince Arthur on 20 May 1872. The following day he also officially opened the Southern Hospital, which was paid for by a fair held at Sefton. The hospital cost £13,000. Total receipts from the fair were £25,035, which left a tidy profit after expenses of £4,984 had been met. An admission charge raised £5,967, the bazaar £12,134 and refreshments £3,243.

WIDNES, BY THE MERSEY 1923 73918

Though hardly a seaside resort, there would be enough activity on the Mersey and the Ship Canal for anyone sitting on the benches to while away a couple of hours.

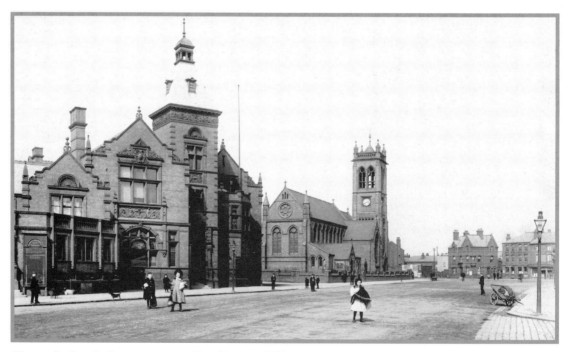

WIDNES, ST PAUL'S CHURCH AND THE FREE LIBRARY 1908 59503

Typical Victorian philanthropy resulted in this prestigious library for the benefit of the working people of the town. Dignified and imposing, it dominates the broad thoroughfare with its stone setts.

WARRINGTON, BRIDGE STREET c1955 W29060
Woodhouse's store has recently opened in what was previously Singleton's. The shop received a new frontage and a complete refit. It was also in Bridge Street that John Howard lodged when printing his work on prison reform.

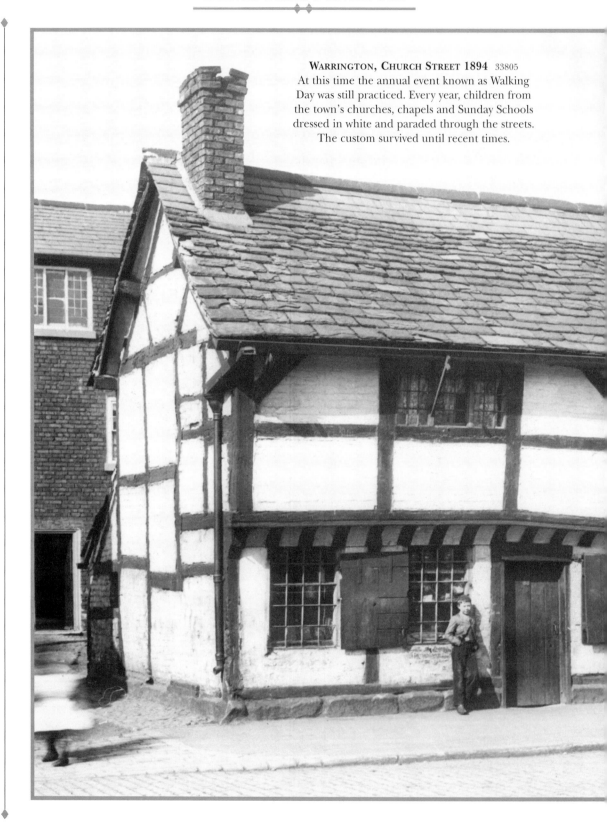

WARRINGTON, CHURCH STREET 1894 33805
At this time the annual event known as Walking
Day was still practiced. Every year, children from
the town's churches, chapels and Sunday Schools
dressed in white and paraded through the streets.
The custom survived until recent times.

WARRINGTON, BUTTERWALK 1894 33806
This photograph features Joseph Beswick's Ye Old Fox Tobacco Stores. Does this unusual name suggest that this building was once an inn? Its strong, stylised lettering is a wonderful example of the signwriter's art.

WARRINGTON, THE TOWN HALL, NEW GATES 1895 36688
The ornamental gates at the entrance to the Town Hall had only recently been erected when this picture was taken. Probably the most interesting monument in the town is the altar tomb of Sir John and Lady Butler who were murdered in 1463. One of the effigies is of their black servant, who managed to save the life of the murdered couple's infant son.

WARRINGTON, THE SWING BRIDGE C1960 W29056
These days, whenever the Chester Road and Northwich Road swing-bridges are opened to allow ships to pass along the Manchester Ship Canal, Warrington grinds to a halt; cars, buses and lorries tail back for hundreds of yards either side of the crossing points. When this picture was taken, things weren't so bad. In the background is the Latchford high-level road-bridge.

GRAPPENHALL, THE CANAL c1955 G200001
The Knutsford Road swing-bridge lies open to allow the passage of a ship, outward-bound from Manchester. In the background is the Latchford railway viaduct, constructed in 1893. For several months after its completion the viaduct was used for freight trains only; the original line being retained for passenger traffic until the last possible moment.

NEW BRIGHTON, THE PIER AND PARADE 1892 30416
In 1830 a retired builder from Everton, by the name of James Atherton, bought 170 acres of sand hills on the northern tip of the Wirral with the express aim of creating a new seaside resort to rival Brighton, hence its name of New Brighton. When the town was first laid out, it was to be an exclusive place, but within a few years cheap, terraced houses had been built and Atherton's vision was in tatters.

NEW BRIGHTON, THE FORT 1886 14269
Fort Perch Rock and the lighthouse. Construction of a fort to defend the seaward approach to Liverpool was first proposed during the Napoleonic Wars, but it was never built because there were arguments as to who should pay for it. Designed by Capt John Kitson of the Royal Engineers, the fort was finally built between 1826 and 1829, at a cost of £27,000.

NEW BRIGHTON, THE LIGHTHOUSE 1887 20069
Built of Anglesey granite, with each stone shaped
by hand, the 90ft tall lighthouse cost £27,000 to
construct. Its light is visible at fifteen miles.

NEW BRIGHTON, THE BEACH AND PIER c1960 N14024

An in-bound Manchester Liner eases her way past New Brighton pier towards the entrance to the Manchester Ship Canal. The ferry service between the pier and Liverpool ceased in 1971 due to silting in the Mersey estuary, and from then on the pier struggled. Supports rotted away, and it was eventually declared unsafe and closed.

NEW BRIGHTON, THE FRONT c1960 N14035

New Brighton was only fifteen minutes away from Liverpool by ferry, and in the summer season it was possible to take trips from here to Llandudno and Ireland. There were two-hour pleasure cruises along the Mersey, which in those days heaved with the ships of the Blue Funnel Line, Glen Line and Elder Dempster.

NEW BRIGHTON, THE TOWER AND SANDS 1900 45163
Based on Blackpool Tower, New Brighton's was built between 1897 and 1900 at a cost of £120,000. At 62ft, it was much higher than Blackpool's, and was the tallest structure in Britain. The Tower's career was somewhat short, however. Neglected throughout the Great War, it was declared unsafe in 1918, and demolition began the following year.

NEW BRIGHTON, THE BEACH 1887 20067
Though the photographers' stalls were harmless enough, the
beach by this date had acquired a reputation for cheap and tacky
sideshows, gambling, brawling and drunkenness. In the
background is Fort Perch Rock. Local fishermen could always earn
their beer money after the fort had fired off a few practice shots by
salvaging the cannon balls and selling them back to the army.

NEW BRIGHTON, GENERAL VIEW 1892 30418

Already, New Brighton is heading down-market and away from James Atherton's ideals. Cheap and tatty eating houses dominated Aquarium Parade to such an extent that it was known better as Ham and Eggs Parade. In 1905, the Corporation succeeded in buying the Parade and immediately demolished it.

WALLASEY, HIGH STREET c1960 W164063

In 1801 the village of Wallasey had 663 inhabitants. By 1851 it had risen to 8,339, and by 1951 it was 101,369, making it the third largest town in Cheshire.

WALLASEY, THE CHURCH AND TOWER c1873 8468
St Hilary's is one of only eight churches in the country dedicated to the saint. There was a church on this site in
the 10th century, and after the Conquest it was rebuilt several times. The lone tower dates back to its rebuilding in
the 1530s; the rest of the church was demolished in 1760. The church in the background was rebuilt in 1858-59
after the previous one had been destroyed by fire.

WALLASEY, TOWN CENTRE c1965 W164082

The old village centre of Wallasey reveals a typical pattern of piecemeal development over the course of a century or more. There are Victorian and Edwardian shops with steep gables and bay windows and plainer infill from the post-war period.

EGREMONT, THE LANDING STAGE 1890 24427

John Askew, who was at one time Liverpool's harbour master, founded the Egremont ferry service. The service finally closed in 1941 after the pier was badly damaged when a ship collided with it.

EGREMONT, KING STREET 1912 64429
A tram rattles down King Street. Both Birkenhead and Wallasey Corporations operated their own tramway systems. Birkenhead's was electrified in 1901 and ran until 1937. Wallasey's operated from 1902 to 1933.

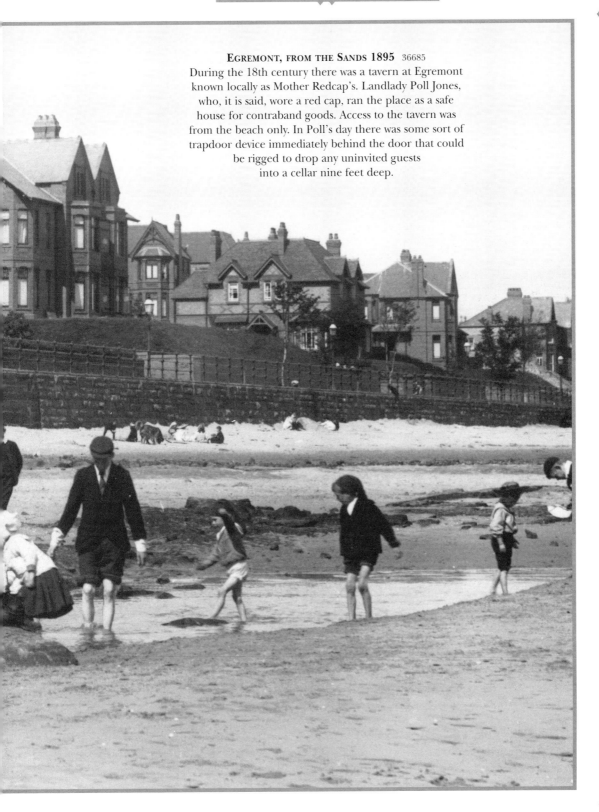

EGREMONT, FROM THE SANDS 1895 36685

During the 18th century there was a tavern at Egremont known locally as Mother Redcap's. Landlady Poll Jones, who, it is said, wore a red cap, ran the place as a safe house for contraband goods. Access to the tavern was from the beach only. In Poll's day there was some sort of trapdoor device immediately behind the door that could be rigged to drop any uninvited guests into a cellar nine feet deep.

EGREMONT, THE FERRY BOAT 1912 64443

EGREMONT
The Ferry Boat 1912
Until 1817 the Mersey ferry service was erratic and subject to the vagaries of wind, tide and weather. In that year the paddle ferry 'Etna' began a regular service between Queen's Dock, Liverpool and Tranmere.

◆

EGREMONT
The Promenade 1898
Along here, just beyond Vale Park, is where the Wallasey Magazines were situated. Built around 1755, the magazines were where vessels using Liverpool were expected to store their powder and shot during their stay in the port. The Magazine Hotel opened in 1759 so that sailors could while away a few hours while they waited to collect their ship's munitions.

EGREMONT, THE PROMENADE 1898 41017

EGREMONT, THE PROMENADE 1912 48662
Egremont was planned by the developer John Askew, a former slave-trader who made his money on land deals involving Liverpool Corporation's unwanted properties in the Wirral. At first, he built himself a house which he named Egremont, after his home town in Cumbria, and the name of the town came from there.

BIRKENHEAD, THE CROSSROADS 1954 B399006
The half-timbered tower belongs to the Halfway House, where Bents' finest ales and stout were served up.

BIRKENHEAD, THE MERSEY TUNNEL c1965 B399027
During construction of the tunnel and its approaches, a large number of Birkenhead's 19th century streets were demolished, though the old parish church of St Mary's was initially spared. With a dwindling congregation, the neglected St Mary's was declared unsafe in 1970, and demolished in 1974.

BIRKENHEAD
Hamilton Square and City Hall c1965
Hamilton Square was laid out in 1826 by Gillespie Graham on the lines of an Edinburgh square. The Town Hall was modelled on that at Bolton, and was completed in 1883, though it was damaged by fire in 1901.

◆

BIRKENHEAD
The Docks c1965
The original plan for the docks involved building a wall across the mouth of Wallasey Pool to create a tidal dock, or float. Though the Morpeth and Egerton Docks were completed in the 1840s, work on the Great Float was not started until the Birkenhead and Liverpool Docks were merged under the Mersey Docks & Harbour Board.

BIRKENHEAD, HAMILTON SQUARE AND CITY HALL C1965 B399041

BIRKENHEAD, THE DOCKS C1965 B399036

BIRKENHEAD, WOODCHURCH ROAD 1954 B399002
A typical town street in pre-supermarket days. Along here were branches of both national and Cheshire retailers including Dewhurst the butcher's and Waterworths.

BIRKENHEAD, ARROWE PARK C1965 B399048
The 425-acre Arrowe estate was once owned by Lord Leverhulme, and purchased by Birkenhead Corporation in 1927. The hall was built between 1835 and 1844 by John Shaw, and one of its owners was Captain Otto Shaw. He excelled at that great Victorian sport of hunting anything that moved. His 'bag' is said to have included 600 cattle killed during a nine-day 'hunt'.

PORT SUNLIGHT, POST OFFICE CORNER c1960 P188066
The earlier houses built at Port Sunlight were a mixture of styles. The village also had a pub, the Bridge Inn, which was designed to look like an old coaching inn, but it opened as a temperance hotel. To give Lever his due, he allowed villagers to hold a referendum to see if it should be licensed. The vote was in favour of it selling beer, and Lever, though a staunch teetotaller, went along with the result.

PORT SUNLIGHT, CHRIST CHURCH c1960 P188053
Christ Church is where Lord Leverhulme and his wife, Elizabeth, are buried, as well as their son, the 2nd Viscount, and his wife. The church is known for its bronze effigies by William Gascombe, who also designed the village war memorial.

HALTON, THE CASTLE 1900 45439

Along with Frodsham, Halton was once of strategic importance. These castles commanded the southern shore of the Mersey estuary and controlled vital river crossing points at Runcorn and Hale.

THE SHIP CANAL AND EASTHAM DOCK c1965 M21504

The four-berth oil dock at Eastham, situated alongside the entrance locks to the Ship Canal. Opened in 1954, it could accommodate tankers up to 35,000 grt and was equipped by direct pipelines to the Stanlow refineries. The dock was capable of handling tankers whose size restricted them from entering the canal proper.

RUNCORN, WESTON POINT c1955 R67019

Since the 1820s Runcorn has been a centre for the chemical industry, with factories producing a wide range of products. In 1803 John Johnson opened a small soap factory. Within thirty years Johnson Brothers were manufacturing 36 per cent of the country's soap, and had diversified into coal and chemicals.

RUNCORN, BIG POOL 1923 73906

One hundred years earlier, Runcorn was already linked to Liverpool by a steam river packet service, which operated two sailings every day from George's Dock. The 'Lady Stanley' sailed every day from the south end of the Parade to Weston Point.

RUNCORN, THE DOCKS c1900 R67301
One of the oldest trades handled here was China clay from Cornwall destined for the Potteries. In the 18th century the clay was transferred to river craft for onward shipment via the Weaver Navigation to Winsford; from there it would be transported by road. With the opening of the canal system, it was possible to trans-ship at Runcorn into narrow boats and take the clay directly to the Potteries.

RUNCORN, THE RAILWAY VIADUCT 1900 45433
The London & North Western Railway viaduct over the Mersey. Work began in 1864 to construct a line from Weaver Junction to provide the LNWR with a more direct route from London and Crewe to Liverpool.

RUNCORN, THE TRANSPORTER BRIDGE 1899 43432A
The transporter bridge connected Runcorn with Widnes on the north shore. The transporter remained in use until 1961, when it was replaced by a road bridge.

RUNCORN, WIDNES BRIDGE C1955 R67043

This is the new single-span 1,082ft road-bridge, built between the railway viaduct and the transporter. Once the bridge opened, the transporter, which was one of only three in the country, was decommissioned.

RUNCORN, DEVONSHIRE PLACE C1955 R67044

In 1964 Runcorn's New Town was designated, the aim being to increase the population from 29,000 to 100,000. The development included the construction of Shopping City, which at the time was one of the largest retail centres in the country.

UPTON, THE VILLAGE c1955 U36002

There are over thirty other Uptons scattered around the country, and by 1931 the local natives at this one were displeased with all the confusion it caused. There was a plan to rename the place Overchurch, and the post office even went so far as to have new franks made, but the plan was never carried through.

UPTON, FORD ROAD c1960 U36013

The parish church of St Mary's was paid for by the shipping tycoon, Thomas Inman, who was the founder of the Liverpool, New York & Philadelphia Steamship Co. The church clock is one of six in the country that have an unusual set of chimes. All were made by John Smith & Co, Derby, who are still in business in 1999.

IRBY, THE OLD POST OFFICE c1948 142001

When this picture was taken, the village stocks had long been nothing but a memory. Some years later the stone posts of the stocks were rediscovered, having been used in the construction of a wall. When the wall was demolished as part of a road widening scheme, the posts were salvaged and a replica set put up near the library.

POULTON, THE MARKET PLACE 1895 35617

In 1080 Hugh de Boidele gave Poulton and several other villages to Robert Lancelyn, in return for the services of two knights and two armed men for forty days each year. Once every three years Robert was also required to provide Hugh with four men to work for six days 'to make my outworks at Dodleston'.

ELLESMERE PORT, FLOUR MILLS AND DOCK c1955 E135009

At this date Ellesmere Port was still relatively active, though signs of the decline to come were visible. Over on the right is one of the warehouses that offered covered barge berths; the flour mills are in the background. The maximum dimensions for Shropshire Union canal craft on the Chester-Ellesmere section was 74ft x 14.5ft x 3.25ft.

ELLESMERE PORT, DOCK STREET c1955 E135022

The inhabitants of Ellesmere Port used to celebrate many of the old high days, fairs and revels. Among them were May Day, when streets competed with one another to put on the best procession; Oak Apple Day, which celebrated the escape of Charles II; and the Good Friday 'battle' between the boys of Ellesmere Port and Long Sutton.

ELLESMERE PORT, THE MANCHESTER SHIP CANAL c1955 E135033

Until the construction of the MSC Shropshire Union Canal, craft had enjoyed direct access to the Mersey by means of a sea lock. From 1894 however, the sea lock, complete with its lighthouse designed by Thomas Telford, provided access to the new ship canal only. Canal pleasure craft are allowed onto the MSC, but they must meet standards for seaworthiness, carry insurance, and apply for permission to make passage.

EASTHAM, STANLEY LANE c1955 E9031

Had the first Manchester Ship Canal Bill been successful, the entrance to the canal would have been further down the Mersey at Runcorn. Eastham Dock might never have been built, and the only shipping activity at Eastham would have been the ferry service to and from Liverpool.

EASTHAM, THE CHURCH c1955 E9036

The parish church has a distinctive tower and spire, but then the old county of Cheshire has a remarkable number of interesting church buildings. Among them are the church of St James and St Paul at Marton, one of the oldest surviving longitudinal timber-framed churches in western Europe; and St Mary's Astbury, which has a tower dating back to 1366, with the main body of the church 15th century.

Index

Adelphi Hotel 36

Art Gallery 30

Bold Street 40

Cathedral 25

Church Street 25

Commutation Row 34

Customs House 22–23

Dale Street 37, 38–39

Exchange 34, 36

Free Library 27

George's Dock 21

Knowsley Hall 44

Lime Street 18–19

Mersey Tunnel 40

Overhead Railway 21

Picton Reading Room 30

Quadrant 28–29, 32–33

Royal Liver Building 24

Sefton Park 44, 45

Sessions House 31

Ships 41, 42, 43

St George's Hall 27

St Nicholas Place 20

Synagogue 26

Town Hall 35

AROUND LIVERPOOL

Birkenhead 68, 69, 70

Eastham 81, 82

Eastham Dock 72

Egremont 62, 63, 64–65, 66, 67

Ellesmere Port 80, 81, 82

Grappenhall 52

Halton 72

Irby 79

Manchester Ship Canal 72, 73

New Brighton 53, 5–55, 56, 57, 58–59, 60

Port Sunlight 71

Poulton 79

Runcorn 73, 74–75, 76, 77

Upton 78

Wallasey 60, 61, 62

Warrington 47, 48–49, 50, 51

Widnes 46

Frith Book Co Titles

Frith Book Company publish over a 100 new titles each year. For latest catalogue please contact Frith Book Co.

Town Books 96pp, 100 photos. County and Themed Books 128pp, 150 photos (unless specified) All titles hardback laminated case and jacket except those indicated pb (paperback)

Around Barnstaple	1-85937-084-5	£12.99
Around Blackpool	1-85937-049-7	£12.99
Around Bognor Regis	1-85937-055-1	£12.99
Around Bristol	1-85937-050-0	£12.99
Around Cambridge	1-85937-092-6	£12.99
Cheshire	1-85937-045-4	£14.99
Around Chester	1-85937-090-X	£12.99
Around Chesterfield	1-85937-071-3	£12.99

Around Maidstone	1-85937-056-X	£12.99
North Yorkshire	1-85937-048-9	£14.99
Around Nottingham	1-85937-060-8	£12.99
Around Penzance	1-85937-069-1	£12.99
Around Reading	1-85937-087-X	£12.99
Around St Ives	1-85937-068-3	£12.99
Around Salisbury	1-85937-091-8	£12.99
Around Scarborough	1-85937-104-3	£12.99
Scottish Castles	1-85937-077-2	£14.99
Around Sevenoaks and Tonbridge	1-85937-057-8	£12.99
Sheffield and S Yorkshire	1-85937-070-5	£14.99
Shropshire	1-85937-083-7	£14.99
Staffordshire	1-85937-047-0 (96pp)	£12.99
Suffolk	1-85937-074-8	£14.99
Surrey	1-85937-081-0	£14.99
Torbay	1-85937-063-2	£12.99
Wiltshire	1-85937-053-5	£14.99

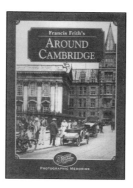

Around Chichester	1-85937-089-6	£12.99
Cornwall	1-85937-054-3	£14.99
Cotswolds	1-85937-099-3	£14.99
Around Derby	1-85937-046-2	£12.99
Devon	1-85937-052-7	£14.99
Dorset	1-85937-075-6	£14.99
Dorset Coast	1-85937-062-4	£14.99
Around Dublin	1-85937-058-6	£12.99
East Anglia	1-85937-059-4	£14.99
Around Eastbourne	1-85937-061-6	£12.99
English Castles	1-85937-078-0	£14.99
Around Falmouth	1-85937-066-7	£12.99
Hampshire	1-85937-064-0	£14.99
Isle of Man	1-85937-065-9	£14.99

British Life A Century Ago
246 x 189mm
144pp, hardback.
Black and white
Lavishly illustrated
with photos from the
turn of the century,
and with extensive
commentary. It offers
a unique insight into
the social history and
heritage of bygone
Britain.

1-85937-103-5 £17.99

Available from your local bookshop or from the publisher

Frith Book Co Titles Available in 2000

Around Bakewell	1-85937-1132	£12.99	Feb
Around Bath	1-85937-097-7	£12.99	Feb
Around Belfast	1-85937-094-2	£12.99	Feb
Around Bournemouth	1-85937-067-5	£12.99	Feb
Cambridgeshire	1-85937-086-1	£14.99	Feb
Essex	1-85937-082-9	£14.99	Feb
Greater Manchester	1-85937-108-6	£14.99	Feb
Around Guildford	1-85937-117-5	£12.99	Feb
Around Harrogate	1-85937-112-4	£12.99	Feb
Hertfordshire	1-85937-079-9	£14.99	Feb
Isle of Wight	1-85937-114-0	£14.99	Feb
Around Lincoln	1-85937-111-6	£12.99	Feb
Margate/Ramsgate	1-85937-116-7	£12.99	Feb
Northumberland and Tyne & Wear			
	1-85937-072-1	£14.99	Feb
Around Newark	1-85937-105-1	£12.99	Feb
Around Oxford	1-85937-096-9	£12.99	Feb
Oxfordshire	1-85937-076-4	£14.99	Feb
Around Shrewsbury	1-85937-110-8	£12.99	Feb
South Devon Coast	1-85937-107-8	£14.99	Feb
Around Southport	1-85937-106-x	£12.99	Feb
West Midlands	1-85937-109-4	£14.99	Feb
Cambridgeshire	1-85937-086-1	£14.99	Mar
County Durham	1-85937-123-x	£14.99	Mar
Cumbria	1-85937-101-9	£14.99	Mar
Down the Severn	1-85937-118-3	£14.99	Mar
Down the Thames	1-85937-121-3	£14.99	Mar
Around Exeter	1-85937-126-4	£12.99	Mar
Around Folkestone	1-85937-124-8	£12.99	Mar
Gloucestershire	1-85937-102-7	£14.99	Mar
Around Great Yarmouth			
	1-85937-085-3	£12.99	Mar
Kent Living Memories	1-85937-125-6	£14.99	Mar
Around Leicester	1-85937-073-x	£12.99	Mar
Around Liverpool	1-85937-051-9	£12.99	Mar
Around Plymouth	1-85937-119-1	£12.99	Mar
Around Portsmouth	1-85937-122-1	£12.99	Mar
Around Southampton	1-85937-088-8	£12.99	Mar
Around Stratford upon Avon			
	1-85937-098-5	£12.99	Mar
Welsh Castles	1-85937-120-5	£14.99	Mar
Canals and Waterways	1-85937-129-9	£17.99	Apr
East Sussex	1-85937-130-2	£14.99	Apr
Exmoor	1-85937-132-9	£14.99	Apr
Farms and Farming	1-85937-134-5	£17.99	Apr
Around Horsham	1-85937-127-2	£12.99	Apr
Ipswich (pb)	1-85937-133-7	£12.99	Apr
Ireland (pb)	1-85937-181-7	£9.99	Apr
London (pb)	1-85937-183-3	£9.99	Apr
New Forest	1-85937-128-0	£14.99	Apr
Scotland	1-85937-182-5	£9.99	Apr
Stone Circles & Ancient Monuments			
	1-85937-143-4	£17.99	Apr
Sussex (pb)	1-85937-184-1	£9.99	Apr
Colchester (pb)	1-85937-188-4	£8.99	May
County Maps of Britain			
	1-85937-156-6 (192pp)	£19.99	May
Around Harrow	1-85937-141-8	£12.99	May
Leicestershire (pb)	1-85937-185-x	£9.99	May
Lincolnshire	1-85937-135-3	£14.99	May
Around Newquay	1-85937-140-x	£12.99	May
Nottinghamshire (pb)	1-85937-187-6	£9.99	May
Redhill to Reigate	1-85937-137-x	£12.99	May
Scilly Isles	1-85937-136-1	£14.99	May
Victorian & Edwardian Yorkshire			
	1-85937-154-x	£14.99	May
Around Winchester	1-85937-139-6	£12.99	May
Yorkshire (pb)	1-85937-186-8	£9.99	May
Berkshire (pb)	1-85937-191-4	£9.99	Jun
Brighton (pb)	1-85937-192-2	£8.99	Jun
Dartmoor	1-85937-145-0	£14.99	Jun
East London	1-85937-080-2	£14.99	Jun
Glasgow (pb)	1-85937-190-6	£8.99	Jun
Kent (pb)	1-85937-189-2	£9.99	Jun
Victorian & Edwardian Kent			
	1-85937-149-3	£14.99	Jun
North Devon Coast	1-85937-146-9	£14.99	Jun
Peak District	1-85937-100-0	£14.99	Jun
Around Truro	1-85937-147-7	£12.99	Jun
Victorian & Edwardian Maritime Album			
	1-85937-144-2	£14.99	Jun
West Sussex	1-85937-148-5	£14.99	Jun

FRITH PRODUCTS & SERVICES

Francis Frith would doubtless be pleased to know that the pioneering publishing venture he started in 1860 still continues today. More than a hundred and thirty years later, The Francis Frith Collection continues in the same innovative tradition and is now one of the foremost publishers of vintage photographs in the world. Some of the current activities include:

Interior Decoration

Today Frith's photographs can be seen framed and as giant wall murals in thousands of pubs, restaurants, hotels, banks, retail stores and other public buildings throughout the country. In every case they enhance the unique local atmosphere of the places they depict and provide reminders of gentler days in an increasingly busy and frenetic world.

Product Promotions

Frith products have been used by many major companies to promote the sales of their own products or to reinforce their own history and heritage. Brands include Hovis bread, Courage beers, Scots Porage Oats, Colman's mustard, Cadbury's foods, Mellow Birds coffee, Dunhill pipe tobacco, Guinness, and Bulmer's Cider.

Genealogy and Family History

As the interest in family history and roots grows world-wide, more and more people are turning to Frith's photographs of Great Britain for images of the towns, villages and streets where their ancestors lived; and, of course, photographs of the churches and chapels where their ancestors were christened, married and buried are an essential part of every genealogy tree and family album.
A series of easy-to-use CD Roms is planned for publication, and an increasing number of Frith photographs will be able to be viewed on specialist genealogy sites. A growing range of Frith books will be available on CD.

The Internet

Already thousands of Frith photographs can be viewed and purchased on the internet. By the end of the year 2000 some 60,000 Frith photographs will be available on the internet. The number of sites is constantly expanding, each focussing on different products and services from the Collection.
Some of the sites are listed below.

www.townpages.co.uk
www.icollector.com
www.barclaysquare.co.uk
www.cornwall-online.co.uk

For background information on the Collection look at the three following sites:

www.francisfrith.com
www.francisfrith.co.uk
www.frithbook.co.uk

Frith Products

All Frith photographs are available Framed or just as Mounted Prints, and can be ordered from the address below. From time to time other products - Address Books, Calendars, Table Mats, Postcards etc - are available.

The Frith Collectors' Guild

In response to the many customers who enjoy collecting Frith photographs we have created the Frith Collectors' Guild. Members are entitled to a range of benefits, including a regular magazine, special discounts and special limited edition products.

For further information: if you would like further information on any of the above aspects of the Frith business please contact us at the address below:
The Francis Frith Collection, Frith's Barn, Teffont, Salisbury, Wiltshire England SP3 5QP.
Tel: +44 (0) 1722 716 376 Fax: +44 (0) 1722 716 881 Email: uksales@francisfrith.com

To receive your FREE Mounted Print

Cut out this Voucher and return it with your remittance for £1.50 to cover postage and handling. Choose any photograph included in this book. Your SEPIA print will be A4 in size, and mounted in a cream mount with burgundy rule lines, overall size 14 x 11 inches.

Order additional Mounted Prints at HALF PRICE (only £7.49 each*)

If there are further pictures you would like to order, possibly as gifts for friends and family, acquire them at half price (no additional postage and handling required).

Have your Mounted Prints framed*

For an additional £14.95 per print you can have your chosen Mounted Print framed in an elegant polished wood and gilt moulding, overall size 16 x 13 inches (no additional postage and handling required).

---

* IMPORTANT!
These special prices are only available if ordered using the original voucher on this page (no copies permitted) and at the same time as your free Mounted Print, for delivery to the same address

---

Voucher for FREE and Reduced Price Frith Prints

Picture no.	Page number	Qty	Mounted @ £7.49	Framed + £14.95	Total Cost
		1	**Free of charge***	£	£
			£	£	£
			£	£	£
			£	£	£
			£	£	£
			£	£	£
			* Post & handling		£1.50
Book Title			**Total Order Cost**		£

Please do not photocopy this voucher. Only the original is valid, so please cut it out and return it to us.

I enclose a cheque / postal order for £ . . . .
made payable to 'The Francis Frith Collection'
OR please debit my Mastercard / Visa / Switch / Amex card

Number . . . .

Expires . . . . Signature . . . .

Name Mr/Mrs/Ms . . . .

Address . . . .

. . . .

. . . .

. . . .

. . . . Postcode . . . .

Daytime Tel No . . . .   Valid to 31/12/01

Frith Collectors' Guild

From time to time we publish a magazine of news and stories about Frith photographs and further special offers of Frith products. If you would like 12 months FREE membership, please return this form.

Send completed forms to:
The Francis Frith Collection, Frith's Barn, Teffont, Salisbury, Wiltshire SP3 5QP

The Francis Frith Collectors' Guild

Please enrol me as a member for 12 months free of charge.

Name Mr/Mrs/Ms . . . .

Address . . . .

. . . .

. . . .

. . . . Postcode . . . .

Free Print - see overleaf